OFFICIALLY
WITHDRAWN

The Missions of California

Mission
San Luis Rey de Francia

Jennifer Quasha

PowerKids Press™
New York

Published in 2000 by The Rosen Publishing Group, Inc.
29 East 21st Street, New York, NY 10010

Copyright © 2000 by The Rosen Publishing Group, Inc.

First Edition

Photo and Illustration Credits: pp. 1, 14, 25, 30, 31, 32, 33, 34B, 35, 36, 45B, 47, 48, 50, 51 © Cristina Taccone; pp. 4, 6, 38 © SuperStock; p. 5 © Stock Montage; pp. 7, 40, 45A © CORBIS/ Bettmann; pp. 9, 42, 44 © North Wind Picture Archive; pp. 10, 28, 29 by Tim Hall; pp. 13, 15, 23 © Michael K. Ward; pp. 16, 21, 46 © The Bancroft Library; p. 17 © The Bridgeman Art Library; p. 19A © The Granger Collection; p. 19B © Gil Cohen; pp. 20, 24 © Seaver Center for Western History Research, LA County; p. 34A, 49 © Shirley Jordan; pp. 39, 41, 43 © Santa Barbara Mission Archive-Library.

Book Design: Danielle Primiceri
Editorial Consultant Coordinator: Karen Fontanetta, M.A., Curator, Mission San Miguel Arcángel
Editorial Consultant: Mary Whelan, Curator, Mission San Luis Rey de Francia
Historical Photo Consultants: Thomas L. Davis, M.Div., M.A. and Michael K. Ward, M. A.

Quasha, Jennifer.
    The Mission of San Luis Rey de Francia / by Jennifer Quasha.
        p. cm. — (The missions of California)
    Includes index.
    Summary: Discusses the mission of San Luis Rey from its founding in 1798 to the present day, including the reasons for Spanish colonization in California and the effects of colonization on the Luiseño Indians.
    ISBN 0-8239-5504-4 (lib. bdg.)
    1. San Luis Rey Mission (Calif.)—History Juvenile literature. 2. Spanish mission buildings—California— Oceanside Region—History Juvenile literature. 3. Franciscans—California—Oceanside Region—History Juvenile literature. 4. California—History—To 1846 Juvenile literature. 5. Luiseño Indians—Missions— California—Oceanside Region—History Juvenile literature. [1. San Luis Rey Mission (Calif.)—History. 2. Missions—California. 3. Luiseño Indians—Missions. 4. Indians of North America—Missions—California. 5. California—History—To 1846.] I. Title. II. Series.
F869.S397Q37 1999
979.4'98—dc21
                                                         99-20441
                                                           CIP

Contents

1   The Spaniards' First Steps: Arrival in California   5
2   The Luiseño Indians   12
3   Founding Mission San Luis Rey de Francia   17
4   Building the King of the Missions   22
5   Education and Daily Life at Mission San Luis Rey de
    Francia   27
6   The Expansion of Mission San Luis Rey de Francia   30
7   The Mission Buildings and Grounds   34
8   Secularization of Mission San Luis Rey de Francia   39
9   The Modern-Day Mission   48
10 Make Your Own Mission San Luis Rey de Francia   52
    Important Dates in Mission History   58
    Glossary   59
    Pronunciation Guide   61
    Resources   62
    Index   63

The Spaniards' First Steps: Arrival in California

Mission San Luis Rey de Francia

At the edge of the busy city of Oceanside, California, is an oasis of calm. Rising high into the blue sky of a quiet inland valley is the bell tower of the church of Mission San Luis Rey de Francia. Beside the church, covering six acres of land, is the rest of the large mission complex. Mission San Luis Rey de Franica was founded in the 1700s by Spanish friars and soldiers, and built by the Luiseño Indians. It stands today as a reminder of the historic beginnings of the state of California and of California's importance in the history of the United States.

The Spanish Come to the Americas

Although Mission San Luis Rey de Francia was not founded until 1798, its story began much earlier. In 1492, after Christopher Columbus brought back news of the Americas to Spain, the Spanish government wanted to explore these lands further. Europeans had never been to the Americas before, and they did not know what they would find there. They went hoping to discover gold, great cities to conquer, or a faster trade route to Asia, where they could buy silks and spices to sell for high prices in Europe.

▲ Columbus claimed the Americas for Spain.

In 1519, a Spanish soldier and explorer named Hernán Cortés brought ships, guns, horses, and soldiers to the land that today is

Mission San Luis Rey de Francia was founded in 1798 and is the largest of the 21 California missions.

Cortés and his army conquered the land that today is Mexico.

Mexico. There, in 1521, he conquered the great Aztec empire for Spain. Spain named the Aztec land New Spain and set up a government under an official called a viceroy, who would act in place of the king. The Spanish quickly established towns in New Spain, but they wanted to expand their empire even more. In 1542, Viceroy Mendoza of New Spain sent an explorer named Juan Rodríguez Cabrillo up the Pacific coast to look for a river that cut through North America to Asia. The Spanish hoped that this would be the trade route they had dreamed of and that it would bring them great riches. Cabrillo did not find this trade route. (In fact, there is no river that crosses all of North America.) Instead, he found the harbor that is known today as San Diego Bay. Harbors were important because they allowed ships to get close enough to shore to let the crew get out and explore the land. When Cabrillo returned to New Spain, he told of the harbor he had found and the land that he had explored. Since Cabrillo hadn't found riches, the viceroy didn't think that the land sounded valuable. He didn't think it was worth the money and effort it would cost to send more ships there. The Spanish would not return to the place they called Alta (meaning "upper") California for many years.

When the viceroy of New Spain finally did send more men to Alta California, it was because he had heard that the Russians were planning to settle there. The Spanish did not want to lose the land they had claimed to the Russians. They decided to send Spanish settlers to Alta California so the Russians would see that the land belonged to the Spanish. On January 9, 1769, the first of three ships set out for the San Diego harbor Cabrillo had found over 200 years earlier. Four months later, on May 15, a group of men began their journey on horseback over land to meet the ships. These men would be the first Spanish colonists in Alta California.

Alta California

Baja California

New Spain

The Mission System

When the Spanish established New Spain in the land that today is Mexico, they learned a lot about settling, or colonizing, a country where people already lived. The Spanish discovered that colonizing an area was easier if they set up missions. A mission is a place where religious leaders go to teach others about their religion. By sending missionaries to teach people in the Americas about Spanish religion and culture, they could get these people to begin to think and act more like the Spanish. Because of this, people in the Americas would not try as hard to fight against the Spanish, and Spain would have an easier time colonizing the land.

The European Worldview

At this time, most Europeans did not value cultural diversity. They believed that their religion and way of life were superior to those of the American Indians. They thought that the Indians needed their help to become more "civilized." These beliefs led them to think of the Indians as children or "savages" that needed to be educated. Because of this, they also believed that they could take away the Indians' land. Today we know that all cultures are important and should be respected. Although the Spanish may have believed that they were helping the American Indians, European colonization of the Americas would eventually destroy the American Indians' way of life.

Establishing Territory

In order to make the newly conquered territory truly Spanish, it needed to be filled with Spanish people. Since the population in Spain was not large enough to bring very many people over to the Americas, the government only sent a few Spanish people, who would encourage the American Indians to become Spanish citizens. This was the goal of the Spanish mission system. The plan to create new Spanish citizens in Alta California required cooperation between two groups: Franciscan friars and the Spanish military.

The Franciscans

At this time, the Spanish were Catholics. The men they sent as missionaries when they colonized Alta California were a group of Catholics called Franciscan friars. Catholics are Christians who follow the pope, who is the head of the Catholic Church. Franciscan friars are members of a special group of Catholics that follows the example of Saint Francis of Assisi, who lived simply and taught his religion to others. Friars, called *frays* in Spanish, take a vow of poverty and agree to devote their lives to the church. The friars who came to California were very religious men who were willing to suffer many hardships to do what they felt their god wanted them to do.

▲
Saint Francis of Assisi was the role model for all Franciscan friars.

Although the Spanish government wanted to build missions to claim more land and create more citizens for Spain, the Franciscan friars went to the missions because they wanted to help the American Indians. They thought that anyone who did not believe in their religion would be punished after he or she died. The friars left their homes and families to travel to the faraway land of Alta California because they hoped that by teaching the American Indians to accept Christianity, they could save the Indians' souls.

Fray Junípero Serra

One of the men who traveled on the May 15 journey to Alta California was a Franciscan friar named Junípero Serra. Serra was born in Spain in 1713 and moved to New Spain to be a missionary, which is someone who teaches others about his religion.

Serra was a devoted friar who dedicated his life to teaching people in the Americas about Catholicism. He was chosen as the president of the Alta California mission system and founded nine missions in the region. Fray Serra died in 1784.

Junípero Serra was the first president of the Alta California missions.

Fray Fermin Lasuén

After Fray Serra died, Fray Fermin Francisco de Lasuén became the president of the Alta California missions. He was in charge of making sure that all the missions had what they needed and were doing well. He was also responsible for founding new missions. During his 18 years as president, Lasuén founded nine missions along the Alta California coast. Mission San Luis Rey de Francia was the last mission that Fray Lasuén founded.

The Soldiers

The Spanish government knew that many California Indians might try to fight against the people who were invading their land. Therefore, the government sent Spanish soldiers to the new territory with the Franciscan friars. Throughout the growth and spread of the California missions, soldiers were used to protect the missionaries from California Indians who might attack them.

Some soldiers lived at military camps, called presidios. Soldiers from the presidio could be called to a mission if the missionaries there needed their help. In addition to the soldiers at the presidio, five soldiers usually lived at each mission. They were there to protect the friars and to make sure that the Indians at the mission did their work. The soldiers often beat or locked up California Indians who did not do as they were told.

The Missions of California

Between July 16, 1769, and July 4, 1823, 21 missions, including Mission San Luis Rey de Francia, were built along the coast of California. The missions were connected by a road called El Camino Real, or the Royal Road. The missions were about 30 miles apart from one another, a distance that took a full day on horseback to travel. The missions brought much that was valuable to California, but they brought many problems as well. The struggles that took place at the missions of California over land, work, and beliefs are struggles that are an important part of all of America's history.

The Luiseño Indians

The Luiseño Name

Before the Spanish arrived to build Mission San Luis Rey de Francia, there were several California Indian villages in the area. When the Spanish came, they called the people who lived in these villages the Luiseños, after the mission's namesake, Saint Louis. Spanish colonization of California would change the Luiseño way of life forever, but before the arrival of the Europeans, the Luiseño culture thrived.

Life Before the Missions

The Luiseño Indians lived much like other California Indians before the arrival of the missionaries. Their homes were made of tree branches covered with mud, and they did their cooking outdoors. The men wore little or no clothing, and the women wore aprons, which tied around the waist and had panels that hung down in front and back. The Luiseños wore sandals made from yucca tree fibers. When it was cold, both men and women covered themselves with warm capes made of rabbit fur or deerskin.

Hunting and Fishing

The Luiseño men were hunters. They were responsible for finding food for their families and for others in the tribe. They used bows and arrows to hunt small game like rabbits and birds. Their bows were made of wood and strung with rope woven from flax and hemp. The shafts of their arrows were made from wood. Their arrowheads were made of hard stone, chipped to form a sharp point. Feathers were attached to the shafts of the arrows to make them fly fast and straight toward their targets. The Luiseños

California Indians lived in small villages. ▶

ate the meat of the animals they hunted and used the skin and feathers as clothing or decoration.

Luiseño men also fished for food. They built boats that were similar to canoes, called *pauhits*, out of wood. These *pauhits* were used for both fishing and travel. Fish were caught with spears or with nets that the Luiseños fashioned out of hand-woven rope.

Gathering and Preparing Food

Like the men, the Luiseño women also provided food for the family. Women gathered seeds, grasses, acorns, and berries to eat. They prepared and cooked the family's meals.

A Luiseño basket.

Acorns were a staple of the Luiseño diet. They were used to make a kind of porridge and to make breads. The acorns were knocked from oak tree branches with large sticks and gathered in baskets. After the acorns had been collected, the women laid them out to dry in the sun. Acorns have poison in them, so they could not be eaten right away. To make the acorns safe to eat, women ground them between two stones, called a mortar and pestle. Then they poured boiling water over the crushed acorns 10 times. This removed the poison, making the acorns ready for cooking.

Luiseño Children

Luiseño boys and girls did not go to school. Instead, they learned from their parents and others in the tribe. Once they were old enough to share some of their tribe's responsibilities, such as hunting, gathering, or caring for younger family members, they took on some of these important jobs themselves.

Arts and Crafts

The Luiseños painted and made crafts. They painted rocks and the walls of nearby caves. They made their paints from mixtures of crushed berries, clays, and dried herbs. Using sticks as brushes, they created pictures of the life around them.

The Luiseños made beautiful necklaces and bracelets from shells and stones they found at the beach and decorated with feathers.

▲
The Luiseños painted walls.

Religion

The Luiseños believed in a religion called Chungiehnish. They believed that their gods watched over them and would punish or reward them for their actions.

The Luiseños held their religious ceremonies in a building called a *wamkish*. When a ceremony was held, people would gather around the *wamkish* to dance and sing. Dancing and singing were important parts of the Luiseño religion. People sang and danced for occasions like births, deaths, and when boys and girls became adults.

The Luiseño culture thrived for hundreds of years before the Spanish came to California. With the arrival of the Spanish, their traditional way of life would be destroyed forever.

Founding Mission
San Luis Rey de Francia

Choosing a Site

In 1769, Fray Juan Crespí, one of the first Spanish friars to arrive in California from New Spain, came upon a green valley five miles east of the Pacific Ocean. Amazed by the beauty of the land, Fray Crespí decided it was a gift from God. He suggested that it be chosen as a site for a mission.

At the time, Mission San Juan Capistrano lay to the north of this valley, and Mission San Diego de Alcalá lay to the south. There were many Indian villages in between these two missions. Travel from one mission to the other was unsafe because it was more than a day's journey, and the Spanish did not like to travel through Indian territory at night.

The governor of Alta California, Governor Borica, decided that a mission should be founded in the area between the two existing missions. This way, Spanish travelers would have a safe stopping point. On February 27, 1798, he sent soldiers from the San Diego presidio to help the president of the missions,

Saint Louis

San Luis Rey de Francia is Spanish for Saint Louis, king of France. Mission San Luis Rey de Francia was named after the French king, Louis IX, who lived in the 1200s. Louis IX led two crusades to spread the Catholic religion to other countries. Much like the California missions' founding friars, Louis IX dedicated his life to spreading the Catholic faith.

◀ *Mission San Luis Rey de Francia was built to close a gap between two existing missions.*

Fray Lasuén, find a suitable site and build temporary shelters there. A spot was chosen, and on June 13, 1798, Fray Lasuén officially founded Mission San Luis Rey de Francia.

The Founding Ceremony

The founding of Mission San Luis Rey de Francia was led by Fray Lasuén. There to witness it were Fray Antonio Peyri, who had come to live at the mission, Captain Grajera and his soldiers from the San Diego presidio, Fray Santiago and a few neophytes from the nearby Mission San Juan, and many Luiseño Indians from nearby villages.

Captain Grajera announced to the crowd that he was taking the land "for the Crown." This meant that he was taking the land for King Carlos III of Spain and that the land would

○ San Francisco de Solano
○ San Rafael Arcángel
○ San Francisco de Asís
○ San José
○ Santa Clara de Asís
○ Santa Cruz
○ San Juan Bautista
○ San Carlos Borromeo del Río Carmelo
○ Nuestra Señora de la Soledad
○ San Antonio de Padua
○ San Miguel Arcángel
○ San Luis Obispo de Tolosa
○ La Purísima Concepción
○ Santa Inés
○ Santa Bárbara
○ San Buenaventura
○ San Fernando Rey de España
○ San Gabriel Arcángel
○ San Juan Capistrano
○ San Luis Rey de Francia
○ San Diego de Alcalá

18

▲

The founding ceremony.

now belong to the Spanish government. Then Fray Lasuén placed a cross in the ground and sprinkled holy water on the earth. This was to show that the place was sacred. Fray Lasuén sang a Mass and gave a sermon.

After the founding ceremony, Fray Lasuén baptized 29 Luiseño girls and 25 Luiseño boys. Baptism is the ceremony that makes someone a Christian. After the Indians were baptized, the friars called the newly converted Indians neophytes. This is an ancient Greek word meaning newly-planted. It was used to mean someone who had just joined the Christian religion. Since Fray Lasuén was in Alta California to convert as many Indians as possible to Christianity, he must have been very pleased with his early success. The missionaries already had many people who wanted to come and live with them at Mission San Luis Rey de Francia, and it was only the first day.

▲

Baptizing a California Indian.

In addition to the children, 19 Luiseño adults also asked to be baptized after the founding ceremony. Fray Lasuén told them that they would have to wait and learn more about the Christian religion first. Since the adults had grown up believing in the Luiseño religion, he felt that they needed to know more about Catholicism before they could be baptized. The children were young, so Fray Lasuén baptized them first so that they could grow up as Christians at the mission.

The First Friars at Mission San Luis Rey de Francia

After founding Mission San Luis Rey de Francia, Fray Lasuén remained there for six days to help Fray Peyri, who would be the mission's leader. Together they decided where grain would be planted, and where the church and friars' quarters would be built. After about a week, another friar, Fray José Faura, arrived at the mission to help Fray Peyri. Fray Peyri was the mission's senior friar. He would be responsible for teaching the Spanish language and the Catholic religion to the Luiseño Indians. Fray Faura would oversee the work that needed to be done outside, such as farming and building.

▲
The friars brought Spanish goods to the Luiseños.

Fray Peyri

While other friars would come and go, Fray Peyri stayed at Mission San Luis Rey de Francia for more than 30 years. He led the mission's development from its founding in 1798, until 1832, when control of the mission had been taken from the friars and given to the government. Fray Peyri had many jobs at the mission. He was at times a teacher, architect, musician, caretaker of the sick, administrator and priest.

Fray Peyri was well respected for many reasons. Unlike some friars, he was friendly to whomever he met. The neophytes at the mission liked him for his kindness and good cheer. He was very energetic, which helped him make Mission San Luis Rey de Francia the largest of the California missions. Fray Peyri had many good qualities, but it is for his talent as an architect that he is most remembered. He began building Mission San Luis Rey de Francia soon after the founding. From there, he oversaw the mission's expansion, which included the church, many buildings, fields, orchards, and an irrigation system that brought water from a nearby river to the mission. Under Fray Peyri's leadership, work on the mission was ongoing. By the time of secularization, the buildings of Mission San Luis Rey de Francia covered almost six acres, making it the largest of the 21 missions.

▲

The grounds of Mission San Luis Rey de Francia.

▲

The mission's garden.

21

Building the King of the Missions

The Mission's Setting

The site of Mission San Luis Rey de Francia, like all the mission sites, was chosen because it had three important elements: rich soil for growing crops, a convenient water supply, and a large California Indian population nearby that could be converted to Christianity and made into Spanish citizens.

A Simple Beginning

Fray Peyri and Fray Faura began their mission with only 12 plowshares, 6 crowbars, some blankets, pickaxes, and cloth to make clothes for the neophytes. Food supplies and livestock were sent from nearby missions to help the friars get started. The friars encouraged the nearby Luiseños to work for the mission by giving them food and blankets in return for their labor.

Upon their arrival, the Spanish missionaries and soldiers built temporary huts as quickly as they could. The Luiseño Indians who had been attracted to the founding ceremony also helped with the work. The temporary shelters were constructed mainly from sticks and mud, and were only meant to last until more permanent structures could be built. To make the shelters, branches were placed in the ground to form walls. Then clay was patted into the sticks to make the walls sturdier and to fill in any holes that would have allowed wind or rain to pass through. Roofs were made from sticks, mud, and thatch or tule, a strawlike reed that could be found on the banks of nearby rivers. Along with this first group of temporary mission buildings, the missionaries built a chapel from the same basic materials.

The friars often worked with the neophytes to build the mission. ▶

Buildings Made to Last

Once the temporary shelters were built, the Spanish missionaries could begin to think about all the things they would need in order to create a successful permanent community at the mission. The buildings that now make up Mission San Luis Rey de Francia would be built over many years. The living quarters and the church were the first permanent buildings to be constructed, since the friars felt that these were the most important buildings at the mission.

The mission's walls were made of adobe bricks. Masons and artisans came from other missions to teach the Luiseño Indians how to make adobe out of a mixture of mud, straw, and water. This mixture was placed into rectangular wooden molds and left to dry in the sun. Once dry, the bricks could be removed from the molds and stored for later use. By July 1, 1798, only one month after the mission's founding, 6,000 adobe bricks had already been made for the mission buildings.

A Successful Start

Life at Mission San Luis Rey de Francia continued to be busy and productive. The Luiseños were working hard at farming and building, and the friars were teaching the Luiseños about Christianity. On August 29, 1798, Fray Lasuén reported to the governor of Alta California that 147 Luiseño Indians had been baptized at Mission San Luis Rey de Francia and that

The Luiseños worked hard.

the friars had married 28 couples in Christian ceremonies. Work was going well, and three rooms of the mission complex were already completed. As president of all the missions, it was Fray Lasuén's job to keep track of how successful the mission was and to help if the people there were having problems. Fray Lasuén was happy that the missionaries at Mission San Luis Rey de Francia were accomplishing so much in such a short amount of time.

Work continued steadily, and, in 1798, the walls of the friars' quarters and soldiers' barracks were finished and had roofs made of thatch and mud. More adobe bricks had been made for the quadrangle. The walls of the *monjerío*, or living quarters for unmarried women and girls, were finished, but no roof had been put up yet because of heavy rains.

By the end of 1798, 214 neophytes already lived at the mission. The mission had 162 cows and bulls, 600 sheep, 28 horses, and 10 mules. Most of these animals had been given to the friars by the leaders of other missions, and they allowed the work of ranching and farming to begin. Mission San Luis Rey de Francia was off to a productive start.

The rooms in the mission had only the most basic furnishings. Fray Peyri's room would have contained a bed made of wooden planks, a wooden chair, and a trunk in which he stored his clothes, books, and a few private belongings.

25

Education and Daily Life at Mission San Luis Rey de Francia

Education of the Luiseño Indians

Daily life at Mission San Luis Rey de Francia revolved around the construction of the mission buildings, farming and other work, and the education of the Luiseño neophytes. The education of the neophytes had two goals. One was to teach them a trade or craft that would be useful at the mission. The missionaries, craftsmen from other missions, and soldiers taught the Luiseños skills like farming, weaving, leather-making, and cooking. The neophytes were used as cheap labor to produce goods that would help improve life at the mission. The friars did not pay the Luiseños for their work. Instead, they provided them with food, some clothing, and shelter. This was much cheaper than paying the Luiseños for the jobs they did.

The other goal of the education of the neophytes was to teach them the Catholic religion and the Spanish language and culture. The friars wanted to teach the Indians about Catholicism because they thought that everyone should believe in the Christian god. The government in New Spain wanted the missionaries to teach the California Indians about Catholicism because they felt that the more the Indians could be made to think and act like the Spanish, the easier it would be for Spain to stay in control of the Californias.

A Loss of Freedom

When the Luiseños came to Mission San Luis Rey de Francia, they had to leave behind their own culture and learn an entirely new way of life. They had to wear new clothes, learn a new language, and live in a new environment. The Luiseños were used to fishing for their own food and only

◀ *The Luiseños became excellent craftspeople.*

producing what the tribe needed. Often, they did not want to follow the strict schedule at the mission or to produce food and other goods for a much larger community.

Once baptized, the neophytes lost their freedom and had to do what the friars told them to do. Neophytes could not leave the mission unless they had special permission. If they tried to flee, they were caught and brought back by the soldiers. Sometimes, they were beaten and punished by the soldiers or friars.

The friars saw the Luiseños as children who needed to be educated and disciplined. The Luiseños were not children though, and they deserved more respect than they often got from the missionaries. The missionaries often behaved toward the neophytes as Spanish parents might have behaved toward their children. According to Spanish custom, the unmarried women and girls were locked in the *monjerío* at night. Any neophyte who did not finish his work might be beaten or locked up.

Beginning in 1799, the friars allowed the neophytes to elect *alcaldes*, or guards. The *alcaldes* were neophytes who communicated between the friars and the neophytes. They were also in charge of making sure that other neophytes were doing their work and following the friars' rules. The *alcaldes* beat anyone who worked too slowly or did not listen to the friars.

Work at the Mission

Despite their loss of freedom, many neophytes stayed and worked at the mission. Mission San Luis Rey de Francia became a center of industry and agriculture. Crops included orange trees, grape vines, wheat, and hemp. The neophytes used wooden plows to till the land and plant their food. They raised cattle for beef and leather, sheep for meat and wool, and hogs for lard, which was used to make soap. Other skills the Luiseño men were taught included adobe brick making, carpentry, tile making, and leatherwork and tanning. Women learned to cook, sew, weave, make soap, and care for the sick. Girls were taught how to spin wool, flax, and cotton.

Neophytes using a plow.

A Typical Day

Daily life at Mission San Luis Rey de Francia was full of activity. Bells were rung at sunrise to wake the neophytes. Everyone gathered for morning prayers and to hear a Mass. After Mass, the friars taught the neophytes lessons on the Catholic religion before breakfast. Everyone then ate breakfast together. After the morning meal, all missionaries, soldiers, and neophytes either set to work or went to classes. At noon, they all came together again for lunch. Lunch was followed by a *siesta*, or rest period, until two o'clock in the afternoon. After the *siesta*, everyone went back to work until sunset, when everyone gathered again at the church for prayers. After prayers came the evening meal, and from then until bedtime the neophytes had free time to dance, play, and talk together.

This strict routine ensured that the mission community was very productive. There were always people cooking, gathering crops, mending walls, making clothes, milking cows, studying their lessons, picking fruit, weaving baskets, cleaning, teaching children, and aiding the sick.

The Expansion of Mission San Luis Rey de Francia

The Building Continues

By the end of the year 1800, even more buildings had gone up at Mission San Luis Rey de Francia. The thatch and mud roof on the *monjerío* had been finished, and there were new rooms for each of the six guards, rooms for the neophyte boys, a weaving room, and three new storerooms. The mission now had 450 cows and bulls, 1,600 sheep, 146 horses, and 14 mules. There were 337 neophytes living at the mission, and even more Luiseño Indians wanted to join. It was partly Fray Peyri's cheerful personality and partly the impressive growth of the mission and the steady supply of food it produced that made so many Luiseños want to live there.

In 1801, a large granary was built to store grain, more rooms were completed, and roofs were put up. The neophytes began to make tile roofs instead of using thatch, sticks, and mud. The red roof tiles were made out of clay that was cut into pieces, rounded over logs, and then baked in a kiln. The tile roofs were strong and served as a shield from the weather. They were better than the thatch roofs that had covered the temporary buildings because they did not catch fire as easily.

▲

Red roof tiles like these were made starting in 1801.

Mission San Luis Rey de Francia. ▶

The Mission Church

By 1802, the mission church was finished. It was a large structure that was 138 feet long, 19 feet wide, and 17 feet high. Fray Peyri made the church large because he wanted to make sure that there would be enough room at Mass for everyone who wanted to join the community at Mission San Luis Rey de Francia.

Inside of the Mission Church

Once the mission church was completed, Fray Peyri turned his attention to having the inside decorated. Details that could not actually be built into the structure, like floral designs, were painted on the walls. Brown, yellow, and red paints were made from clay in the soil. Other colors were made from minerals imported from Spain.

A few years after the church was finished, the friars were able to get

a crucifix, a statue of Saint Louis, an oil painting of Jesus Christ being baptized, and some silver religious objects for the inside of the church.

This original statue of Saint Louis
◀ *was brought to the mission in 1808. It still stands in the church today.*

Mission San Luis Rey de Francia's church altar is decorated with colorful paintings and statues.

The Mission Buildings and Grounds

The Quadrangle

Mission San Luis Rey de Francia is the largest of the 21 missions.

▲

Plants in the garden.

▲

The arches.

Because of this, it was called the "King of the Missions." Like the other missions, Mission San Luis Rey de Francia was built in the shape of a quadrangle, or hollow rectangle. By 1804, all the buildings that formed the quadrangle were completed. The quadrangle at Mission San Luis Rey de Francia is 500 by 500 feet, the size of two football fields put together. Inside the quadrangle is a courtyard that once contained gardens and work areas.

By 1811, the mission population had grown so large that a bigger church was needed. Construction on the church began, and the neophytes worked on it until 1815, when it was completed. This church, which still stands today, is 175 feet long, 28 feet wide, 30 feet high, and could hold up to 1000 people. The church forms the east side of the mission complex. The mission buildings that formed the square around the courtyard included the friars' quarters, the boys' dormitories, the *monjerío*, workshops,

Mission San Luis Rey de Francia. ▶

storage rooms, and the infirmary, where the sick were cared for. There were also many buildings outside of the mission quadrangle, including storehouses, soldiers' barracks, mills, tanneries, workshops, and many of the neophytes' homes in the *ranchería*.

▲

The gargoyle.

The Irrigation System

Within the mission's six acres of land was an irrigation system that took water from a nearby river and distributed it throughout the mission grounds. This meant that the neophytes did not have to leave the mission to get water for washing, cooking, and drinking. It was also used to bring water to the plants in the gardens. The mission's *lavandería*, or open-air laundry, had a fountain for washing and bathing. Water

▲

The lavandería *with its gargoyle fountain.*

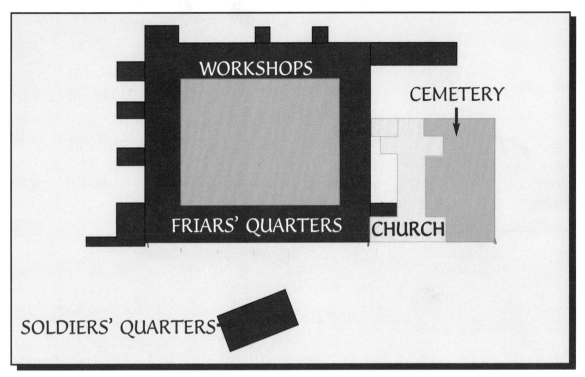

WORKSHOPS

CEMETERY

FRIARS' QUARTERS

CHURCH

SOLDIERS' QUARTERS

flowed from the mouth of a gargoyle. Some of the water from the *lavandería* was drained into the sunken garden to water the plants and fruit trees.

Peyri's Design

Though it was the Luiseño Indians who actually built Mission San Luis Rey de Francia, the architectural design was Fray Peyri's. Since Fray Peyri was Spanish, the style of the mission is like some of the architecture in Spain. All of the missions share similar features of open courtyards with gardens or a fountain, terraced bell towers, red tile roofs, and arched corridors. The design of Fray Peyri's Mission San Luis Rey de Francia was a masterpiece of architectural design, as well as an impressive example of the skill of the Luiseño builders.

P: Vancouver

L. Eel   L. of the   L.Puce
L. Sturgeon   Woods
White   Bear L.
Bear L.   Falls of St Anthony
R. St Peter

Lake Superior

Mishipicotor Nipissing
L.

CAN

L. Huron

N. Wabash   PENI

UNIT

Missouri R.   Moin R.

Mississippi River

St Francis
Puerto de Monterrey
P. Estero
Leyzao   Sta Fe
Ouiquimoc   NEW
S. Pedro
S. Felipe   LOUISIANA
Yumas   MEXICO
S. Marie
NAVARRE F. Yanos   Rio Colorado
Nacora   St Paul   Texas
St Antonia   Cenis   New Orleans
Lorello

Akansas
New Madrid
R. St Francis

Black R.
Red R.
Trinity R.
Arkansas

Upper
Creeks

R. Ohio
Lexington
KENTUCKE
TENNESSE
STAT

Augusta
S. CARO
GEOR
Dario

W. FLORIDA
Mississippi
River

C St Blas
Apalacha B.
Spirito Santo
Charlotte B.
Chatham

GULF

OF

MEXICO

Velicato
CALIFORNIA
L Cerros
ro Hermoso
B. Magdalena

GULF OF CALIFORNIA

St Juan Baptista
la Conception
Sinaloa
Culiacan
Culiacan

C St Lucas
Marias I.
C. Corientes

Conception
Andoe
Cuasteca
Panuco

Guaynamota
Compostella
Mechoacan
Mechoacan

P. de St Jot

Zacatula

Acapulco
Port Escondido
Port Aguanlepec
Tecoanlepec

Rio Bravo
B. Nassas

MEXICO

L. Blanche

P. Piedra
Mt Delgado
Campeche
Mexico
B. of Campeche

St Bernard

Guzaca
St Ildeconza

Cidad Real
or
NEW SP

MEXICO

Martyr
Ha

C. Antonio
Cotoche
Merida
Cosumel I.
Ambergrease I.

BAY OF HONDU
Rattan I.
Hon

Truxillo
Cape

St Salvador
St Miguel

Port Remedios

Secularization of Mission San Luis Rey de Francia

An End to Help from New Spain

In 1810, the people in New Spain began to fight for independence from the Spanish government. Since there was a war going on, no more money or supplies were sent from New Spain to the missions. The friars at Mission San Luis Rey de Francia had to make sure that the neophytes could make or trade with others for everything that they needed. The missions were also forced to supply soldiers at nearby presidios with food, even though the people at the missions needed the food themselves.

During this difficult time, Fray Carranza, the friar who was at Mission San Luis Rey de Francia with Fray Peyri, wrote to Fray Lasuén to ask for permission to return to New Spain. Mission life was difficult, and the friar felt isolated from his home and culture. Fray Lasuén sent a friar named Gerónimo Boscana to replace Fray Carranza, and Fray Carranza went home. Two more friars came and went between 1811 and 1823, but Fray Peyri remained faithful to Mission San Luis Rey de Francia.

▲
Gerónimo Boscana.

California Becomes Part of Mexico

In 1821, New Spain won its independence from Spain and became Mexico. California now belonged to Mexico instead of Spain. The Mexican government decided to break up the California mission system and take the buildings and land from the Franciscans. Taking the mission lands away from religious leaders and placing them under

◀ *Today, Mexico is an independent nation.*

control of the Mexican government was called secularization.

Secularization of the Mission

When the missions were secularized on July 25, 1826, Governor Echeandia of Mexico said that he was freeing the California Indians at some of the missions, including Mission San Luis Rey de Francia. Since the government was now in control of the missions, he said that friars should only perform religious duties like giving Masses and sermons. After the neophytes at Mission San Luis Rey de Francia heard that they were free, some of them refused to work for the mission anymore.

Although the governor said that he had freed the neophytes from the missions, the Indians still had to obey Mexican government officials. On January 6, 1831, Governor Echeandia appointed a military officer named Captain Pablo de la Portilla to go to Mission San Luis Rey de Francia to divide up the mission lands and give 33 acres to each adult male over 20 years of age.

Portilla told the neophytes they were free, but this was not really true. The Mexican government had made it legal to force the California Indians to work in the fields. Captain Portilla tried to make the neophytes at Mission San Luis Rey de Francia work, but after a month at the mission he

▲

Even during the difficult time of secularization, many neophytes came to live at Mission San Luis Rey.

reported, "These Indians will do absolutely no work nor obey my orders." The Luiseños shouted at him, "We are free! We do not want to obey! We do not want to work!"

Even with some of the problems caused by secularization, in 1831, Mission San Luis Rey de Francia was at the most successful point in its history. It had 26,000 cattle, 25,500 sheep, 300 pigs, 1,300 goats, and 2,150 horses. In the same year, the neophytes harvested 395,000 bushels of grain and produced 2,500 barrels of wine. From dawn to dusk, the inhabitants of the mission led busy lives. Fray Peyri drew many Indians to the mission and encouraged them to be baptized. In 1831, Mission San Luis Rey de Francia had 2,800 Luiseño Indians living and working within its boundaries.

Fray Peyri Departs

Fray Peyri was very upset by the changes taking place at Mission San Luis Rey de Francia, but he did not have the power to stop the Mexican government. Because of the fighting with Spain, in 1829, Mexico had said that all men under 60 years old who were born in Spain would have to leave Mexican lands, including Alta California. Fray Peyri tried to get special permission to stay, but permission was denied. Fray Peyri would have to leave the mission.

On January 17, 1832, after 34 years of service, Fray Peyri left Mission San Luis Rey

▲
Fray Peyri was well-loved by many neophytes at the mission.

de Francia. He sneaked out at night in an effort to avoid saying a difficult good-bye to the neophytes. The following morning, when the neophytes awoke, Fray Peyri was gone. One story says that 500 Luiseños mounted their horses and rode to the port of San Diego. They arrived just as Fray Peyri's ship was backing away from the dock. Many Luiseño Indians jumped into the water and swam out to the ship to beg him to return, but it was useless. Fray Peyri, filled with regret, was on his way back to Spain. Standing on deck with outstretched hands, Fray Peyri blessed them and said his final good-byes. It is

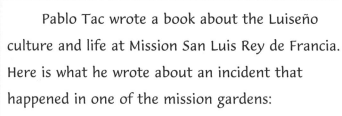

Pablo Tac wrote a book about the Luiseño culture and life at Mission San Luis Rey de Francia. Here is what he wrote about an incident that happened in one of the mission gardens:

"Once a neophyte entered the garden without knowing the gardener was there. He was very hungry so he climbed a big fig tree. Here he began to eat with all haste a large ripe fig. Not by bits but whole he let it go down his throat, and the fig choked him. He then began to be frightened, until he cried out like a crow and swallowed it. The gardener, hearing the voice of the crow, with his Indian eyes found the crow that from fear was not eating anymore. He said to him, 'I see you, a crow without wings. Now I will wound you with my arrows.' Then the neophyte with all haste fled from the garden."

said that for years after his departure, the Luiseño Indians prayed for Peyri's return.

Fray Peyri brought two Indian boys with him to Spain, Pablo Tac and Agapito Amamix. Both boys were brought to Rome and sent to a school to become friars. Both boys died of illness before they could finish school. Agapito Amamix died in 1837. Pablo Tac died in 1840.

Problems at Mission San Luis Rey de Francia

Secularization caused many problems at Mission San Luis Rey de Francia. Without the cheerful, friendly, and skillful leadership of Fray Peyri, the neophytes were not interested in staying at the mission. In addition, they were angered by the Mexican officials who tried to make them work. Two friars, Fray Antonio Ánzar and Fray Vicente Pasqual Oliva had been sent to take Fray Peyri's place as leaders of the mission. Fray Oliva became depressed and almost crazed by the events at Mission San Luis Rey de Francia. There was no order at the mission, no one was working, the neophytes stopped attending religious services, and the soldiers were drinking and gambling with the neophytes.

The Mission Changes Hands

In 1834, the mission was surrendered to the Mexican government. The Luiseño Indians were scattered throughout the area. Secularization called for changing the

▲
Fray Antonio Ánzar.

43

missions into towns, called *pueblos*. The Mexican government hoped that the California Indians would live in these *pueblos* as tax-paying Mexican citizens. Most of the time, this did not happen. Many of the Luiseño Indians at Mission San Luis Rey de Francia did not stay at the mission very long after its secularization. Once the friars left the mission, the Luiseños were not interested in keeping the mission running or in maintaining its way of life.

Although the Mexican government tried to pass laws to help the Luiseño Indians set up life for themselves on the mission's land, some corrupt officials wanted the land for themselves. In 1846, Mission San Luis Rey de Francia, which was worth more than $200,000, was sold by the

▲
Pio Pico.

Mexican governor, Pio Pico, to members of his family for only $2,437. After the mission was sold, it was stripped of all its valuable goods. The property was divided, and the mission was abandoned. It was not occupied again until the Mexican War, when U.S. troops, including the Mormon Battalion, lived there. The mission finally became part of the United States in 1850 when California became a state. The United States had won the Mexican War and claimed this territory as part of its victory.

Mission San Luis Rey de Francia Is Returned

On March 16, 1865, less than one month before he was assassinated, President Abraham Lincoln returned Mission San Luis Rey de Francia to the Catholic church. A copy of this decree, signed by Lincoln, can still be seen at the mission today. There had not been a religious service held in the mission for many years. The quadrangle had fallen to ruin, and the church was damaged.

▲

President Abraham Lincoln.

The mission remained abandoned for the next 30 years, until 1892, when several Franciscan friars from Zacatecas, Mexico, were given permission by the Bishop of California to come to San Luis Rey de Francia to save it. The revival of the mission was led by Friar Joseph Jeremiah O'Keefe. O'Keefe was an Irish-born, Spanish-speaking friar, who wanted to turn the ruined mission into a Franciscan missionary college. O'Keefe and a group of friars began repairing the mission, and it was rededicated on May 12, 1893, by Bishop Mora. For the next 19 years, Friar O'Keefe stayed at the mission to oversee its restoration. By 1905, a smaller, two-story quadrangle was complete. Even after Friar O'Keefe's death in 1915, reconstruction continued at the mission.

▲

This is the decree that Lincoln signed.

▲

Ruins of Mission San Luis Rey de Francia.

The Mission Attracts Attention

By the 1920s and 1930s, the Franciscans had restored the mission enough to allow movies to be filmed there. In 1922, a movie called *The Pride of Palomar* was shot at Mission San Luis Rey de Francia, and the mission became a tourist attraction.

By 1931, the church had been restored closer to the original design of Fray Peyri. Restoration of the soldiers' barracks and the *lavandería*

took place in the 1950s and 1960s. The television show *Zorro* was filmed at the mission in 1957, gaining further publicity for Mission San Luis Rey de Francia. In 1970, the United States Department of the Interior made the mission a National Historic Landmark. This was to protect the mission buildings from being changed or torn down.

Friar O'Keefe began the important work of restoring the mission.

The Modern-Day Mission

The Past Preserved

Today Mission San Luis Rey de Francia is a working mission. There are Masses held every Saturday at 5:30 P.M. in the mission church, where the copper baptismal font made by the neophytes is still displayed. The church's altar is partly original and partly reconstructed. The wooden church doors are hand-carved.

▲

The church doors.

There is a mission museum that shows exhibits of the mission's history, including Luiseño baskets, vestments worn by the 18th and 19th century friars, works of art including a sculpture of Saint Louis, and a display of the mission kitchen. It contains artifacts from all periods of the mission's history, beginning with the Luiseño Indians before the Spanish arrived. It includes objects from the time of Spanish settlement, Mexican secularization, and occupation by the United States military.

The mission kitchen display shows how the kitchen was once used. There are large open grills, on which meat was cooked for hundreds of people. The counter holds baskets and handmade tools that the Luiseño women used in food storage and preparation.

▲

The friars' vestments.

Mission San Luis Rey de Francia. ▶

48

The Cemetery

Mission San Luis Rey de Francia's cemetery dates back to 1798. It is the oldest burial ground in North San Diego County that is still used. Members of the families that helped rebuild the mission are buried there, and the recent expansion of the area will now make it available for use by people of all faiths. There is also an Indian Memorial that was built in 1830 in memory of the Luiseño Indians who helped create the mission and for the many who died there.

A memorial at the cemetery recognizes the many California Indians who lived and worked at Mission San Luis Rey de Francia.

Keeping History Alive

Though the past 200 years have not always been kind to Mission San Luis Rey de Francia, its future looks promising and secure. Many men and women are dedicated to keeping its history alive so that the upcoming generations can learn about California's early history by seeing the inner workings of the King of the Missions.

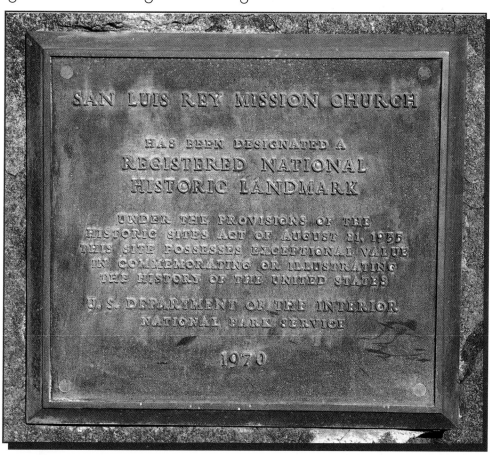

▲

This plaque says that Mission San Luis Rey de Francia was named a landmark in 1970.

Make Your Own Mission
San Luis Rey de Francia

To make your own model of Mission San Luis Rey de Francia, you will need:

foamcore   glue
corrugated cardboard   miniature pots
greenery   miniature bell
Scotch tape   wire
scissors

Directions

Step 1: Use a large piece of cardboard for your base.

Adult supervision is suggested.

Step 2: Cut out two pieces of foamcore that are 3"x 8" and two pieces that are 3" x 6".

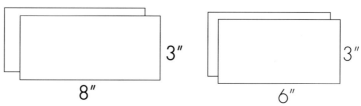

Step 3: Carefully cut arches in one of the 3" x 8" pieces. This will be the front of your mission.

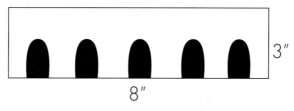

Step 4: Arrange the foamcore pieces so they form a box shape. Tape them together. Attach to the mission base.

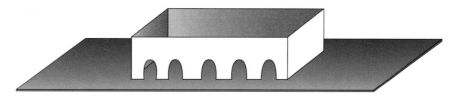

Step 5: Cut out 12 pieces of foamcore that are 2" x 3" and 6 pieces that are 1.5" x 3".

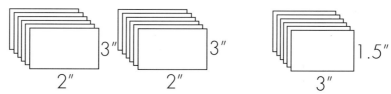

Step 6: Tape two pieces that are 2" x 3" and one piece that is 1.5" x 3" into three sides of a box. Repeat with all pieces to form six three-sided boxes.

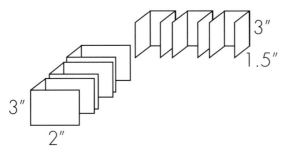

Step 7: Tape three of these box shapes to the right side of the building and three along the back, as shown.

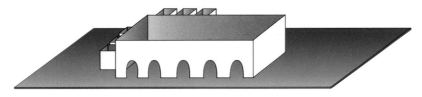

Step 8: To make the church buildings and steeple, cut out three foamcore pieces that are 3" x 3" and six that are 1.5" x 3".

Step 9: Tape together two pieces that are 3" x 3" and one piece that is 1.5" x 3" to form three sides of a box. Attach to the left side of the mission.

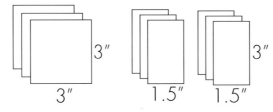

Step 10: Tape together one piece of foamcore that is 3″ x 3″ and one piece that is 1.5″ x 3″ to form an "L" shape. Attach the "L" shape next to the first box.

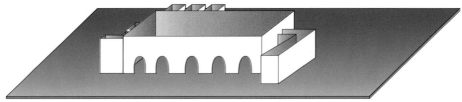

Step 11: To make the church steeple, use the remaining four pieces that are 1.5″ x 3″. Tape together in a square and place on top of the first box.

Step 12: Cut out two pieces of foamcore that are 3″ x 3″ and one piece that is 2″ x 3″. Tape these into three sides of a box and attach to front, right side of the main building.

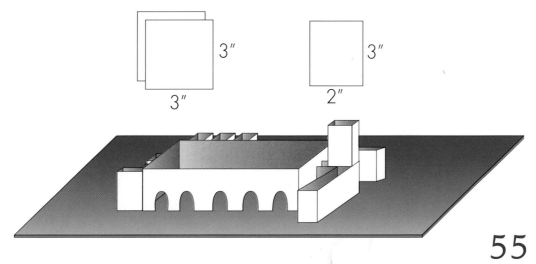

Step 13: To make the roofs, cut out two pieces of cardboard that are 2" x 8" and two pieces that are 2" x 6" for the main building. For the small buildings, cut out roofs that are 2" x 2".

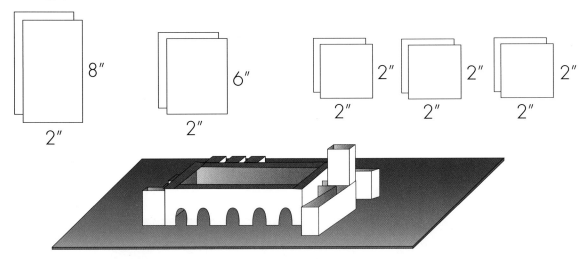

Step 14: For the church building, cut out two roofs that are 3" x 1.5". For the church steeple, cut one piece that is 2" x 4" and fold in half. Attach all pieces and glue in place.

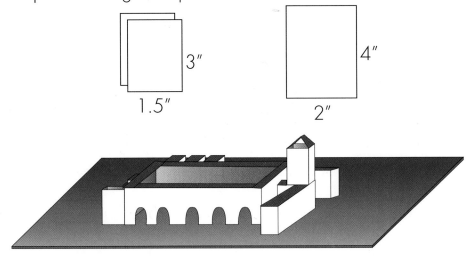

Step 15: Attach a bell to the church steeple. Add miniature pots and fill with greenery. Decorate as you wish.

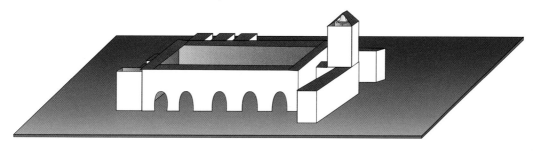

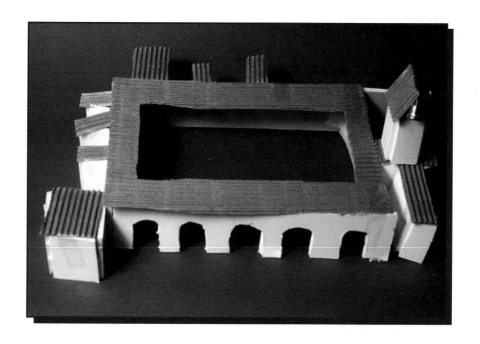

*Use the above mission as a reference for building your mission.

Important Dates in Mission History

1492	Christopher Columbus reaches the West Indies
1542	Cabrillo's expedition to California
1602	Sebastián Vizcaíno sails to California
1713	Fray Junípero Serra is born
1769	Founding of San Diego de Alcalá
1770	Founding of San Carlos Borromeo del Río Carmelo
1771	Founding of San Antonio de Padua and San Gabriel Arcángel
1772	Founding of San Luis Obispo de Tolosa
1776	Founding of San Juan Capistrano
1776	Founding of San Francisco de Asís
1776	Declaration of Independence is signed
1777	Founding of Santa Clara de Asís
1782	Founding of San Buenaventura
1784	Fray Serra dies
1786	Founding of Santa Bárbara
1787	Founding of La Purísima Concepción
1791	Founding of Santa Cruz and Nuestra Señora de la Soledad
1797	Founding of San José, San Juan Bautista, San Miguel Arcángel, and San Fernando Rey de España
1798	**Founding of San Luis Rey de Francia**
1804	Founding of Santa Inés
1817	Founding of San Rafael Arcángel
1823	Founding of San Francisco de Solano
1848	Gold found in northern California
1850	California becomes the 31st state

Glossary

adobe (uh-DOH-bee) Sun-dried bricks made of straw, mud, and sometimes manure.

architecture (AR-kuh-tek-chur) The art of designing buildings.

baptism (BAP-tih-zum) A ceremony performed when someone is accepted into, or accepts, the Christian faith.

barracks (BAYR-iks) A building or set of buildings that are used to house soldiers.

Catholicism (kuh-THAH-lih-sih-zum) The faith or practice of Catholic Christianity, which includes following the spiritual leadership of priests headed by the pope.

Christianity (kris-chee-A-nih-tee) A religion based on the teachings of Jesus Christ and the Bible, practiced by Eastern, Roman Catholic, and Protestant groups.

convert (kun-VIRT) To change from belief in one religion to belief in another religion.

decree (dih-KREE) An official law or order.

Franciscan (fran-SIS-kin) A communal Roman Catholic order of friars, or "brothers," who follow the teachings and example of Saint Francis of Assisi, who did much work as a missionary.

friar (FRY-ur) A brother in a communal religious order. Friars can also be priests.

granary (GRAY-nuh-ree) A building where grain is stored.

irrigation (eer-ih-GAY-shun) To supply with water.

livestock (LYV-stahk) Farm animals kept for use or profit.

Mass (MAS) A Christian religious ceremony.

neophyte (NEE-uh-fyt) The term for American Indians once they had been baptized.

quarters (KWOR-turz) Rooms where someone lives.

ranching (RAN-ching) Raising cattle, horses or sheep on a farm.

restoration (reh-stuh-RAY-shun) Working to return something, like a building, to its original state.

secularization (seh-kyuh-luh-rih-ZAY-shun) When the operation of the mission lands was turned over to the Mexican government.

tanning (TA-ning) Taking animal skins and making them into leather that can be used.

thatch (THACH) A covering for a house made up of reeds and grass bundled together.

vestments (VEST-mints) Robes that are worn for special ceremonies.

viceroy (VYS-roy) A governor who rules and acts as the representative of the king.

villages (VIH-lih-jiz) Original communities where American Indians lived before the arrival of the Spanish.

Pronunciation Guide

alcaldes (ahl-KAHL-dez)

fray (FRAY)

lavandería (lah-vahn-deh-REE-ah)

Luiseño (loo-ih-SAY-nyoh)

monjerío (mohn-hay-REE-oh)

pauhits (POW-eetz)

pueblos (PWAY-blohs)

rancherías (rahn-che-REE-as)

siesta (see-EHS-tah)

wamkish (WAHM-kish)

Resources

To learn more about the California missions, check out these books and Web sites:

Books:

Bleeker, Sonia. *The Mission Indians of California*. New York: William Morrow and Company, 1956.

Oh California. Boston: Houghton Mifflin Co., 1991.

Robinson, Alfred. *Life in California*. Santa Barbara: Peregrin Smith, Inc., 1970.

Web Sites:

California Missions Resource Page
http://www.csd.k12.ca.us/coyote_canyon/4/missions/mission_ndx.html

Spanish Missions of California
http://tqd.advanced.org/3615/

Mission San Luis Rey de Francia
http://www.sanluisrey.org

Index

A
adobe, 24, 25, 29
architecture, 21, 37

B
baptism, 19–20, 24, 28, 32,
    41
Boscana, Gerónimo, 39

C
Cabrillo, Juan Rodríguez, 6, 7
Carranza, Fray, 39
Christianity, 9, 19–20, 22, 24
colonizing, 7, 8–9, 12
Columbus, Christopher, 5
Cortés, Hernán, 5–6
Crespí, Fray Juan, 17

E
El Camino Real, 11
explorers, 5–6

F
farming, 24, 25, 27, 28
Faura, Fray José, 20, 22

I
irrigation system, 21, 36

L
Lasuén, Fray Fermín, 10, 18–20,
    24, 25, 39
livestock, 22, 25, 30, 41
Luiseño Indians, 5, 18, 19–20,
    22, 24, 37, 42, 43, 50
    culture of, 12–15, 48
    life at the mission, 27–29, 30,
        41, 44

M
Mass, 19, 29, 32, 40, 48
missionaries, 8, 9, 10, 11, 12,
    19, 22, 24, 25, 29
    teaching of Indians by, 7, 27
    treatment of Indians by, 28

N
neophytes, 18, 19, 21, 22, 25,
    28, 29, 30, 34, 36, 39,
    42
    secularization, and, 40–41,
        43–44

treatment of, 27–28

O

O'Keefe, Friar Joseph Jeremiah,
45

P

Peyri, Fray, 18, 20–21, 22, 30,
32, 37, 39, 41–43, 47
Portilla, Captain Pablo de la,
40–41
presidios, 11, 17, 18, 39

R

restoration, 46–47

S

Saint Louis, 12, 17, 32, 48
secularization, 21, 40–41,
43–44, 48
Serra, Fray Junípero, 10
soldiers, Spanish, 5, 8, 11, 17,
18, 22, 25, 29, 39, 43
treatment of Indians by, 11, 28